PARTS OF ME:

A Teen's Guide to Exploring the Inner World with Internal Family Systems

Calandra Balfour

GARNSTONE PRESS

Published by Garnstone Press
ISBN 978-1-7393-7492-1

Copyright © Calandra Balfour 2023

Calandra Balfour has asserted her right to be identified as the author of this Work in accordance with the Copyright, Designs, and Patent Act 1988

Dedicated to Tim, Dana, Fi
and Light Before Dawn.

Thank you for the inspiration, for all of the support, for walking beside me, and for the love you show me and all my parts.

CONTENTS

CHAPTER 1 13
GET TO KNOW YOUR TEAM: An Introduction To IFS

CHAPTER 2 21
GETTING TO KNOW YOUR INNER TEAM MEMBERS

CHAPTER 3 31
FEELINGS MATTER: Learning About Feelings

CHAPTER 4 41
SELF ENERGY

CHAPTER 5 47
THE 8 C's OF SELF ENERGY: A Quick Look

CHAPTER 6 53
CARING: The First C is Compassion

CHAPTER 7 61
STAYING COOL: The Second C is Calmness

CHAPTER 8 69
SEEING CLEARLY: The Third C is Clarity

CHAPTER 9 77
ASKING QUESTIONS: The Fourth C is Curiosity

CHAPTER 10 85
BELIEVING IN YOURSELF: The Fifth C is Confidence

CHAPTER 11 93
MAKING THINGS: The Sixth C is Creativity

CHAPTER 12 103
BEING BRAVE: The Seventh C is Courage

CHAPTER 13 113
FEELING CONNECTED: The Eighth C is Connectedness

CHAPTER 14 121
THE 5 P's OF SELF ENERGY: Let's Learn More

CHAPTER 15 125
TAKING YOUR TIME: The First P is Patience

CHAPTER 16 131
BEING PRESENT: The Second P is Presence

CHAPTER 17 137
HAVING FUN: The Third P is Playfulness

CHAPTER 18 145
NEVER GIVING UP: The Fourth P is Persistence

CHAPTER 19 151
LOOKING AT THE BIG PICTURE: The Fifth P is Perspective

CHAPTER 20 159
MAKING FRIENDS WITH YOUR INNER TEAM

CHAPTER 21 171
HEALING AND WELCOMING BACK HIDDEN PARTS

CHAPTER 22 181
GET CREATIVE

CHAPTER 23 189
TIME TO PRACTICE AND REFLECT

APPENDIX 197

AKNOWLEDGMENTS 205

BIOGRAPHY 207

PARTS OF ME

FOREWORD

Life's challenges can be a real puzzle, especially when it comes to understanding our own feelings. That's where 'Parts of Me: A Teen's Guide to Exploring the Inner World with Internal Family Systems' comes in. It's like a toolkit, designed to help young people navigate their emotions and build a healthy inner world.

Based on the pioneering work of Dr. Richard Schwartz, 'Parts of Me' is a friendly guide to the Internal Family Systems (IFS) model. Whether you're a teen, a child, a parent, a therapist, or someone who is simply curious, this book can open doors to the world of IFS.

If you are a practitioner looking to use this with clients, check out the Appendix at the end. It's packed with ways to make the most of this book in your practice.

What makes IFS special? It helps us understand the different 'parts' of our personalities and how to work with them. By embracing these parts, we can create a more balanced inner world, leading to a stronger, happier self. 'Parts of Me' lays out these ideas in a simple and enjoyable way, packed with practical techniques and interactive activities.

If you're a parent using this book with your teen, I invite you to try the exercises yourself first. That way, you can support the whole family in creating a nurturing environment.

What I love about 'Parts of Me' are the creative exercises that encourage readers to explore emotions through art, writing, music, and more. But remember, for those dealing with trauma or severe emotional distress, there is no substitute for a skilled IFS therapist.

So, what can you expect from this guide? Two things. First, it's about helping young people make friends with their internal parts. It sets the stage for deeper exploration when the time is right. Second, it unveils the superpower of Self Energy (trust me, it's fascinating - you'll learn all about it in the following pages).

'Parts of Me' is more than just a book; it's a journey towards self-discovery and growth. As you turn the pages, you'll unlock the power of IFS to transform lives, including your own. Here's to embarking on this exciting adventure towards self-awareness, inner balance, and emotional wellbeing. Thanks for choosing 'Parts of Me' as your guide, and may you and all your parts find balance and growth on this path.

Calandra Balfour

PARTS OF ME

PARTS OF ME - CHAPTER 1

GET TO KNOW YOUR TEAM:
An Introduction To IFS

What is IFS Therapy?

Have you ever felt like there are different voices inside your head, all telling you different things? Maybe one voice tells you to do your homework while another tells you to watch TV instead. Well, this is a normal and common experience that many people have. And that is where Internal Family Systems come in!

Internal Family Systems, or IFS for short, is a therapy that helps people understand and work with the different 'parts' of themselves. These parts are like different voices or aspects of ourselves with different thoughts, feelings, and behaviours. Sometimes these parts can conflict, and cause us to feel overwhelmed or stuck.

But with IFS, we can learn how to identify and understand these parts and work with them in a positive and healthy way. It is a way of understanding and working with the different parts of yourself that make up your inner crew. Doing this makes us feel more balanced, calm, and in control of our thoughts and feelings.

Think of it like a family - and how a family is made up of different people with different personalities, a person is made up of different parts with different personalities. And like in a family, it is important to listen to each part, understand their needs, and work together to benefit the whole. Think of your inner team as a family of characters, each with its own unique personality.

Some of your inner team members are called managers who help you stay organised, safe, and in control. They might come across as the bossy ones. Other members are called firefighters, who help protect you when you feel threatened or stressed by distracting you. Finally, some members are called exiles, these are your hurt parts. They are the parts of ourselves that we are most prone to hide because we don't want to feel the pain or humiliation associated with them. Exiles hold your more vulnerable emotions associated with past wounds and trauma.

Our parts are like different voices or aspects of ourselves with different thoughts, feelings, and behaviours.

IFS is all about learning how to listen to and work with the different parts of yourself, to feel more in control of your thoughts and emotions. It is a powerful tool to support you in navigating life's challenges and feeling more connected to yourself and others. The goal is to help you build a more balanced and harmonious inner world where all your parts can work together towards your goals and dreams. With IFS therapy, you'll learn how to be the captain of your inner team and ensure they are all working together to help you thrive.

Why It is Important to Understand Our Emotions

Our feelings are a huge part of who we are and play a big role in our lives. They can change how we act and think when we're happy, sad, angry, or scared. Sometimes our emotions can be too much to handle or confusing, making life harder to deal with. That is why it is important to understand our emotions and learn how to handle them in a healthy way. By understanding how our feelings work, we can better know what we need and want. This can make us feel better and more satisfied with our lives.

In IFS therapy, understanding our emotions is a big part of working with our inner team. Each part of our personality has its own set of emotions, and when we can understand and accept them, we can better handle them in a healthy way. This can help us get along with ourselves and other people better. By understanding our emotions and working with our inner team, we can get better at knowing ourselves and what we need to feel happy. So, take some time to get to know your inner team and the emotions that come with them – it could be the key to a more fulfilled life!

GETTING PRACTICAL
Getting to Know Your Inner Team

Take a few minutes to check in with yourself and notice how you're feeling. Ask yourself which part of you is feeling the strongest emotions now, and write down or draw the parts that make up your inner crew. There might be an angry part, a happy part, there could even be a bored part. What other parts do you notice?

Can you notice what each crew member wants, needs, or worries about? This exercise can help you build a relationship with your inner team and develop a better understanding of your emotions. Remember, the more you practice, the stronger your connection with your inner team will become.

PARTS OF ME

My Thoughts Today

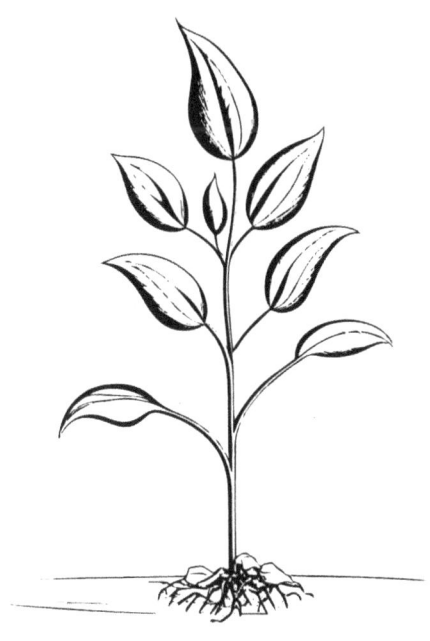

PARTS OF ME

PARTS OF ME - CHAPTER 2

GETTING TO KNOW YOUR INNER TEAM MEMBERS

Introducing The Idea Of 'Parts.'

In the last chapter, we learned about Internal Family Systems and how It is all about understanding the different inner team members - parts of ourselves. In this chapter, we'll dive deeper and find out more about these parts!

First, let's start with the concept of 'parts.' Remember, parts are like different voices or aspects of ourselves with different thoughts, feelings, and behaviours. These parts can be organised into different categories or roles:

- **Managers:** These parts of us try to control everything and keep us safe. They might tell us to study hard, be polite, or avoid risky situations.

- **Firefighters:** These parts of us try to distract us from painful emotions or situations. They might tell us to eat sweets, binge-watch TV, play computer games, spend ages on our phones, or lash out at others.

- **Exiles:** These are the wounded parts of us that hold painful memories, emotions, or beliefs that we've pushed away or tried to ignore. They might be hurt, scared, or ashamed.

PARTS OF ME

You might have more managers than firefighters or more exiles than managers. We'll find out about these different parts in more detail in the following pages. It is important to remember that every person's parts are unique and can vary in number and type. All of your parts are working hard to protect you, they are doing the best they can to protect you. Your parts might change over time, depending on your experiences and what's happening around you.

So, how do you get to know your parts? One way is to focus on your thoughts, feelings, and behaviours. Notice when you feel anxious, angry, or sad, and try to identify which part is responsible that emotion. You can even give names to your parts or draw pictures of them to make them more concrete.

Another way to get to know your parts is to practice mindfulness or meditation. By being in the moment and aware of your thoughts and feelings, you can learn to observe your parts without judging or reacting to them. Remember, getting to know your parts is the first step in working with them and finding balance in your life. So, take some time to explore and get to know your inner world - you might be surprised at what you discover!

Internal Family Systems therapy helps us understand that we have different parts inside ourselves, each with its jobs and personalities. We looked at the three types of parts - manager, firefighter, and exile – but let's find out what they do in more detail.

What are Manager Parts?

One type of part is called a manager part, which takes charge and tries to control situations to keep us from feeling hurt or upset. These parts are like bosses, looking after tasks and ensuring everything goes well.

Manager parts can be very organised, structured, and controlling, always trying to do everything perfectly. They might be critical of themselves and others, ensuring things are done 'right.' They try to avoid feeling upset or vulnerable by focusing on tasks and achievements.

While manager parts can be helpful sometimes, they can also make us feel too controlled and less flexible. We might find it hard to let go or have trouble relaxing and having fun. In some cases, manager parts can even make us work too hard, causing us to feel very tired and worn out.

It is important to remember that our manager parts are there to protect us, and they are not 'bad'. But we may need to work with them to find a better balance. One way to do this is by thanking them for their help and gently showing them that it is okay to let go of control sometimes.

Manager parts can be very organised, structured, and controlling, always trying to do everything perfectly.

In IFS, we try to understand why our manager parts are doing what they do. For example, a manager part might want to protect us from feeling scared or unsure, or they might want to do everything perfectly to make others happy. By understanding their reasons, we can find other ways to meet those needs that are healthier and more balanced.

Another important part of working with our manager is being kind to ourselves. We can learn to thank our managers for their help, while being gentle with ourselves when things are tough. We can remember that we are not just our manager parts; we deserve love and kindness just as we are.

In the end, our manager parts are important, but we need to work with them in the right way. By saying thank you, understanding their reasons, and being kind to ourselves, we can feel more relaxed in our lives.

What are Firefighter Parts?

There is another type of part called firefighter, that help when we feel upset or scared. Firefighters are like superheroes that try to save us from tough emotions by distracting us from the things that make us sad or worried.

Firefighter parts can show up in different ways for different people. Some examples might be eating too many snacks, playing video games for hours, or not talking to friends. These actions might not seem helpful, but they are just the firefighter's way of protecting us from feeling bad.

Sometimes, the things firefighters do can cause problems too. For example, eating too many snacks can give us a stomach-ache, and not talking to our friends might make us feel lonely.

One way to help a firefighter part is to let them know they are not alone. When they learn that there are other parts inside us that can help, they might feel better and try new ways to help us feel safe and happy. Another way to help our firefighters is to understand why they do what they do. By figuring out what makes them act the way they do, we can learn to work with them in a more understanding and caring way.

Firefighters are like superheroes that try to save us from tough emotions by distracting us from the things that make us sad or worried.

Ultimately, our firefighter parts are important helpers when we are upset or scared. But it is important to work with them to find new ways to feel better that don't cause problems. By getting to know our firefighter parts and understanding why they are there, we can create a happier and more supportive team inside us.

What are Exile Parts?

As we've learnt, different parts work together to help us explore the world. But sometimes, some parts can become separated or 'exiled' from the rest, which can make us feel sad or scared. Remembering that these exiled parts are normal in our inner world is important.

Exile parts often hold on to sad memories or feelings we don't want to think about, so we push them away. But ignoring these parts can make things worse. When we don't listen to and understand these parts, they can feel even stronger and more overwhelming. Exile parts often hold on to sad memories or feelings we don't want to think about, so we push them away.

Exiles hold onto to sad memories or feelings we don't want to think about so we push away.

Instead, it is important to notice that these parts are there and treat them with kindness and curiosity. We can start to welcome them back into our inner world by saying 'hello' to them and listening to what they want to tell us. A gentle and slow approach is best with these parts.

GETTING PRACTICAL
Getting to Know Your Inner Team

Draw a picture of yourself and label each part that you can identify. Use colours or symbols to represent each part and write a brief description of what it represents. Don't forget to give them names, so you really get to know them.

PARTS OF ME

Inner Crew Notes

PARTS OF ME

PARTS OF ME - CHAPTER 3

FEELINGS MATTER:
Learning About Feelings

How To Identify and Understand Our Feelings

In the last chapter, we learned about the different parts of ourselves and how they can affect our thoughts, feelings, and behaviours. In this chapter, we are going to focus on one of the most important aspects of our inner world: feelings.

Feelings are powerful and complex, and they can sometimes feel overwhelming or confusing. But understanding and working with our feelings is essential for our wellbeing and happiness in the long-term.

So, what are feelings? Feelings are emotions that arise in response to a situation or event. They can be positive, like happiness, excitement, or love. They can be negative, like sadness, anger, or fear. Feelings can also be a mix of both, like feeling anxious and excited at the same time. Remember that all feelings are valid and normal - there are no 'good' or 'bad' feelings, only different ways of feeling. But sometimes, our parts can try to control or suppress our feelings, which can lead to problems.

That is why it is important to learn how to identify and work with our feelings in a healthy way. Here are some tips for understanding your feelings:

- **Name your feelings:** Try to give them a name whenever you feel an emotion. This can help you identify and acknowledge what you're feeling.

- **Notice the physical sensations:** Feelings can also be felt in the body, so pay attention to any physical sensations you're experiencing (like a tight chest, clenched tummy, or a racing heart).

- **Accept your feelings:** Remember that all feelings are valid and normal; it is okay to feel what you're feeling.

- **Practice self-compassion:** Treat yourself with kindness and understanding, especially when experiencing difficult feelings. It's ok to feel this way, and lots of people feel this way too.

By understanding and working with our feelings, we can learn to be more resilient, compassionate, and in control of our inner world. So, take some time to explore your feelings and learn how to work with them in a positive and healthy way!

Learning how to work with our feelings and make space for them.

Understanding feelings is an important part of our mental

and emotional wellbeing. Feelings can be complex and overwhelming, and it is normal to feel confused or unsure about how to deal with them. But by learning how to work with our feelings and make space for them, we can develop a healthier relationship with them and improve our overall happiness.

The first step to understanding our feelings is to become more aware of them. This means paying attention to how we feel and identifying the feelings we are experiencing. Sometimes, we might feel a mix of feelings, or we might not be sure what we are feeling at all. That is okay – it can take time to develop this awareness.

Once we've identified our feelings, the next step is to make space for them. This means allowing ourselves to feel our emotions without judging or criticising. It can be tempting to push our feelings away or ignore them, but doing that only leads to more discomfort and distress in the long run.

Instead, we can try to approach our feelings with curiosity and openness. We can ask ourselves questions like:

'What is this feeling trying to tell me?'

'What do I need right now?'

By doing this, we can learn more about our feelings and ourselves. It is important to remember that all feelings are valid and okay to feel. There's no 'bad' feeling – even if a particular emotion feels uncomfortable or difficult to deal with. Emotions are simply a part of being human, and we all experience them in different ways.

'What is this feeling trying to tell me?'

'What do I need right now?'

One technique for working with feelings is mindfulness. Mindfulness involves paying attention to the present moment in a non-judgmental way. By practising mindfulness, we can become more aware of our feelings and learn to observe them without getting caught up in them. This can be a helpful way to create space for our feelings and prevent them from overwhelming us.

Another technique is to express our feelings in a healthy way. This might involve talking to a trusted friend or family member, writing in a journal, or engaging in creative activities like art or music. By expressing our feelings in a healthy way, we can release some of the tension and stress they might be causing us.

Learning how to work with our feelings is a process; it takes time and practice. It is important to be patient with ourselves and remember that making mistakes is okay. Developing a healthier relationship with our feelings can improve our mental and emotional health.

GETTING PRACTICAL
Feelings Matter - Learning About Feelings

Make a list of your most common feelings. Write down which part of you usually experiences each one. Can you see a pattern or any recurring themes?

PARTS OF ME

Feeling Friends

PARTS OF ME

Parts of Me Poem

In this book of wisdom, for the challenges we face,
A special way of thinking, we learn to embrace.
Inside our hearts, so strong and bright,
Courage, curiosity, kindness, and love, shining like light.

Life can be tough, and we might feel fear,
Embarrassed or sad, our hearts needing cheer.
To keep them safe, we make friends to defend,
Some helpful, some not, but all there to attend.

Instead of pushing these friends away, let's see,
The reasons they're there, and how they help you and me.
We can find new ways for them to give a hand,
And save the hidden friends we've left in the sand.

On a mission, with our special friends to lead,
We'll make our hearts stronger, yes indeed.
With the help of our protectors, we'll discover,
The hidden parts, and the feelings we used to cover.

As we learn and grow, we'll become even stronger,
Our protectors can rest, they're needed no longer.
We've found a new way to keep moving on,
Freeing our hearts from pain and fear, fears gone.

So let's remember to care for the 'Parts Of me',
With its friends, here the real magic starts – you'll see.
Together, we'll find our hearts' missing links,
And feel happier, stronger, and better, don't you think?

PARTS OF ME

PARTS OF ME - CHAPTER 4

SELF ENERGY

What is Self Energy?

Self Energy is a big idea in Internal Family Systems therapy. It is all about the core of who we are and comprises compassion, calmness, curiosity, and confidence among others. According to IFS, every person has limitless Self Energy, which is always available but can be covered up by different parts of our personality. IFS is about connecting with our Self Energy.

When we are in touch with our Self Energy, we feel a sense of balance and wholeness. It is like a wise leader inside of us that can guide us towards healing and growth. It is not far away or hard to reach - it is a natural part of who we are.

The idea of Self Energy is like other concepts you might have heard of before, like your intuition or inner voice. It is about learning to listen to yourself and trust yourself to make the right decisions. When we are in touch with our Self Energy, we can feel more purposeful and at peace with ourselves.

In IFS therapy, the goal is to help people connect with and strengthen their connection to their Self Energy. This means learning how to work with the different parts of our personality in a way that allows our Self Energy to shine out of us.

One of the cool things about Self Energy is that it is not limited to certain people or cultures. It is something that **everyone** can access and grow, no matter where they come from, or what they believe in. It is all about learning how to listen to yourself and trust yourself to make decisions that are right for you.

Why is it important to learn about Self Energy?

Well, when we are in touch with our Self Energy, we are better able to recognise what we want and need, and we are more confident in our ability to make decisions that are right for us.

Self Energy is like a wise leader inside of us that can guide us towards healing and growth.

Overall, the idea of Self Energy is an important concept to learn about if you're interested in exploring your inner world. By learning how to connect with your Self Energy, you can develop a greater sense of purpose and balance.

Another cool thing about Self Energy is that it is not just a feeling or an idea – it is a set of qualities we can develop and cultivate. By learning to connect with our Self Energy, we can be kinder to ourselves and others, stay calm in tough situations, make the right choices, explore new thoughts and ideas, trust our feelings, and enjoy life with creativity and excitement.

What are some of the characteristics and qualities associated with Self Energy?

Do you ever feel like you have different parts of yourself that want different things? Sometimes it can be hard to understand and manage all of those parts. That is where the 8C's and 5P's of Self Energy come in! Self Energy is the essence of who we are. the part of us that remains unchanged, no matter what is happening in our lives. The 8 C's are qualities that make up our Self Energy, and the 5 P's describe the different characteristics of these qualities in more detail.

The 8C's

Caring.

Calm.

Clarity.

Curiosity.

Confidence.

Creativity.

Courage.

Connectedness.

The 5P's

Presence.

Playfulness.

Persistence.

Perspective.

Patience.

These characteristics work together to create a strong sense of Self that can help us navigate life's ups and downs more easily. By growing the connection to our Self Energy and practising the 8 C's and 5P's, we can develop a deeper understanding of ourselves and our place in the world. In the next chapters, we will dive into the 8C's and 5P's in more detail, so we can understand them better and learn how to use them!

PARTS OF ME

PARTS OF ME - CHAPTER 5

THE 8 C's OF SELF ENERGY:
A Quick Look

A Quick Look

As you may have noticed in the previous chapter, Self Energy is a really important deal in Internal Family Systems therapy. It comprises the 8C's - curiosity, calmness, clarity, confidence, creativity, compassion, connectedness, and courage. When we are in touch with our Self Energy, we feel more balanced, and at peace with ourselves.

The 8C's

1. **Compassion:** being kind and caring to ourselves and our parts, even when things are difficult, or we make mistakes. When we are in touch with our Self Energy, we can better extend compassion to ourselves and our parts. This means that we are more likely to see things from different perspectives or points of view, and we are less likely to judge ourselves or others harshly.

2. **Calmness:** staying cool, staying centred and grounded, even when things get tough, so that we can better cope with challenges. When we connect with our Self Energy, we are better able to stay calm and regulate our feelings, even in tough situations. This can help us feel more in control and less overwhelmed.

3. **Clarity:** seeing things clearly and making decisions that are right for us, even when it is hard to know what to do. When we are engaged with our Self Energy, we are better able to see things clearly and make decisions that are right for us. This means we are less likely to feel confused or unsure about what we want, or need.

4. **Curiosity:** means being open to new experiences and exploring the world with a sense of wonder and interest. It can also mean being curious about what parts we have, and what they want us to know. When we access our Self Energy, we are more likely to approach life with a sense of wonder, ask questions, and explore new ideas and perspectives. This can help us feel more excited and interested in the world around us.

5. **Confidence:** trusting our instincts and being confident in who we are and what we want, even when others don't understand. When we deepen our connection to our Self Energy, we are more likely to trust our instincts and make the right decisions. This can help us feel more confident in our choices and more comfortable in our skin.

6. **Creativity:** using our imagination to develop new ideas and solutions. When we are connected to our Self Energy, we

are more likely to approach life with a sense of playfulness and creativity and to explore new ideas. This can help us feel more inspired and motivated in everything we do.

7. **Courage:** being brave, even when we feel scared or uncertain. As we engage with our Self Energy, we are more likely to have the courage to do tough things, even when we feel scared. This can help us grow and learn new things.

8. **Connectedness:** feeling connected to ourselves, others, and the world around us, and understanding how we are interconnected. As we get in tune with our Self Energy, we are more likely to feel a sense of connection to ourselves, all our beautiful parts, and the world around us. This can help us feel happier in our lives and less alone.

The 8C's are important, so now that we know what they are, let's explore each of them, one by one!

PARTS OF ME

Heartfelt Hopes

PARTS OF ME

PARTS OF ME - CHAPTER 6

CARING: The First C is Compassion

PARTS OF ME

Caring

What is compassion? It means being caring and extending kindness and understanding to ourselves and all our parts. Compassion is an awesome quality that can help us approach life with kindness, empathy, and understanding. It is all about extending this kindness and understanding to ourselves, to all our parts, and others, even when things get tough, or we make mistakes.

One of the best things about compassion is that it allows us to connect more deeply with others and build stronger, more meaningful relationships. When we approach others with kindness and empathy, we are more likely to understand their experiences and feelings and connect with them on a deeper level.

Compassion also helps us be more forgiving and understanding of ourselves and our parts when we make mistakes or experience difficult feelings. Instead of being hard on ourselves, we can learn from our experiences in a more positive way and use them to grow and improve.

Caring for ourself is having an open and understanding

mindset, and being willing to extend this kindness and empathy to ourselves and others, even when it is hard. It means embracing our vulnerability and recognising that we all make mistakes and endure tough times.

Compassion means being kind and caring to ourselves and others, even when things are difficult, or we make mistakes.

One way to grow compassion is to practice self-compassion on a regular basis. This could mean using positive self-talk, mindfulness techniques, or other strategies that help us extend kindness and understanding to ourselves, even when things are challenging.

Another way to develop compassion is to look for opportunities to extend kindness and empathy to others in our daily lives. This could mean volunteering, offering support to friends or family members going through a tough time or simply being kind to someone who looks like they could use a little extra support.

One of the challenges of cultivating compassion is that it can be difficult to extend kindness and empathy to ourselves and our parts when we are feeling stressed or overwhelmed. But by embracing our vulnerability and being kind to ourselves and others even in difficult circumstances, we can develop the compassion we need to lead to be happier.

GETTING PRACTICAL

Here are five questions you can ask yourself to grow compassion:

1. **How can I be kinder to myself?** This question encourages you to treat yourself with the same level of compassion and kindness that you extend to others. It helps you grow a sense of self-care and recognise the importance of self-compassion.

2. **What can I learn from this experience?** This question prompts you to reflect on your experiences, both positive and negative, and recognise opportunities for growth and learning. It helps you recognise that mistakes and challenges in your life can be good, even if it doesn't seem like it at the time.

3. **How would I feel in this person's shoes?** By asking this question, you to take a perspective of empathy and understanding. It helps you recognise the feelings and experiences of others and consider their feelings. It also helps to see things from the point of view of one of your parts.

4. **What can I do to help this person?** With this question you can notice how you could take action and show kindness to others. It helps you recognise opportunities to offer support and assistance to those in need.

5. **How can I make the world a better place?** This question encourages you to consider the impact of your actions and choices on the world around you. It helps you recognise the importance of contributing to a greater good and making a positive difference in the world, no matter how small.

PARTS OF ME

Compassion Chronicles

PARTS OF ME

PARTS OF ME - CHAPTER 7

STAYING COOL:
The Second C is Calmness

PARTS OF ME

Staying Cool

Being calm and cool is a superpower that helps us stay steady, even when things are tough. It is all about staying in the moment and keeping focused, even when we are stressed, worried, or unsure.

When we are cool and calm, we can handle challenges better and make choices that feel right for us. We are less likely to act without thinking or get swept away by our feelings, and we can stay focused on what truly matters.

One of the great things about calmness is that it is contagious. When we can stay calm and centred, our parts stay calm, and we can help others around us feel more grounded and at ease as well. This can help create a positive and supportive environment where everyone feels comfortable and safe.

Cultivating calmness can be challenging, especially when we are facing difficult situations. But there are several things we can do – strategies - to help us stay centred and grounded, even when things get tough.

One strategy is to practice mindfulness. This involves paying attention to the present moment without judgment or distraction. By focusing on our breath, senses, or surroundings, we can help quiet our minds and stay centred in the present moment.

Another strategy is to practice relaxation techniques, such as the deep breathing exercise 'Balloon Breathing' (see below). These techniques can help reduce feelings of stress, feelings of anxiety and can help us feel calmer.

It is also important to take care of our physical health to grow calmness. Getting enough sleep, eating a healthy diet with plenty of fruits and veggies, and engaging in regular exercise can all help us feel more centred and grounded.

Calmness means staying cool, staying centred and grounded, even when things get tough so that we can better cope with challenges.

One of the challenges of cultivating calmness is that it can be easy to get caught up in our feelings and thoughts. We might feel overwhelmed by stress or anxiety or get carried away by our thoughts and feelings. But practising mindfulness and other relaxation techniques can help quiet our minds and stay centred in the present moment.

Overall, calmness is essential to help us navigate life's challenges much easier.

A simple and useful deep breathing exercise is called 'Balloon Breathing.' Here's how to do it:

- Find a comfortable place to sit or lie down with your back straight but relaxed.

- Close your eyes or focus on a spot in the room.

- Imagine you have a balloon in your belly. When you breathe in, the balloon fills up with air; when you breathe out, the balloon deflates.

- Place one hand on your belly, so you can feel it rise and fall as you breathe.

- Take a slow, deep breath through your nose, counting to 4 in your head. Feel the balloon in your belly filling up with air and your hand rising.

- Hold your breath for a moment.

- Slowly breathe out through your nose, counting to 4 in your head. Imagine the balloon in your belly deflating and your hand lowering.

- Repeat this process 5-10 times or until you feel more relaxed and calmer.

- Remember to keep your breaths slow and deep, filling your belly like a balloon. This exercise can help you feel more relaxed and grounded. You can use it whenever you need a moment of calm.

GETTING PRACTICAL

Here are five questions you can ask yourself to grow calmness:

1. **What physical sensations am I feeling right now?** This question helps you become more aware of your body and notice any tension or discomfort. By focusing on physical feelings in your body, you can learn to relax and release tightness.

2. **What thoughts are running through my mind right now?** This question helps you become more aware of your thoughts and feelings. By noticing your thoughts and feelings, you can learn to accept them without judgment and let them pass.

3. **What can I do to take care of myself at this moment?** This question encourages you to prioritise self-care and consider what you need to feel calm and centred. It could be taking a break, going for a walk, or Balloon Breathing.

4. **What is within my control right now?** This question helps you focus on what you can control and let go of what you can't. By focusing on what you can control, you can feel more in control and less worried.

5. **What can I be thankful for at this moment?** This question encourages you to focus on the positive and grow a sense of gratitude. By focusing on what you're grateful for, you can shift your perspective and feel calmer.

PARTS OF ME

Staying Cool

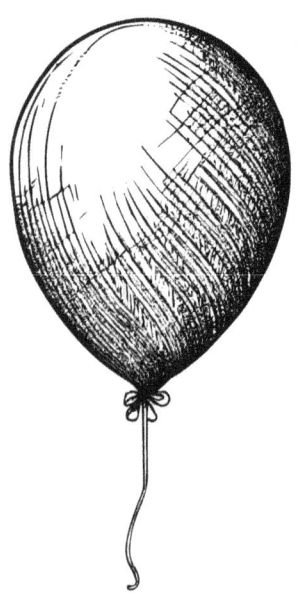

PARTS OF ME - CHAPTER 8

SEEING CLEARLY: The Third C is Clarity

PARTS OF ME

PARTS OF ME

Seeing Clearly

Clarity is a powerful quality that can help us see things clearly and make the right decisions, even in difficult situations. When we are clear about what we want and need, we are more likely to make choices that are good for us.

Clarity is like having a superhero vision. It helps us see through the busy world and stay aware of the situation. When we know our goals, what we care about, and what matters most, we don't get distracted by what our parts might be worrying about. This helps us stay focused and keep going, even when things get tough.

To see clearly, we need to take a step back and think about our lives and our dreams. This means taking time to figure out what we want and what is truly important. It also means being brave enough to let go of things that don't help us, and make changes that might be hard but will make us happier.

Being clear about what we want is like having a superpower. To get better at it, we can try two things: thinking about our thoughts and feelings and talking to people we trust.

First, we can spend some time looking at our thoughts, feelings, and actions to see if we need to change something. By being honest with ourselves and seeing our lives from a different angle, we can understand what we need to do to be our best selves.

Second, we can talk to people who care about us, like friends, family, teachers, or helpers. They can help us see things more clearly and find out where we might be stuck.

Clarity means seeing things clearly and making decisions that are right for us, even when it is hard to know what to do.

In IFS, clarity helps us connect with our inner wisdom and Self Energy. Sometimes, it is not easy to know what we want or need. We might feel confused or unsure about what's important. But if we take time to think, talk to others, and remember what matters most, we can make the right choices for our true selves.

PARTS OF ME

Here are some simple self-reflection questions that can help you better understand your thoughts, feelings, and actions and see more clearly.

- **How am I feeling right now?** Can I name the emotion(s) I'm experiencing?

- **What made me feel this way?** Was it something that happened, something someone said, or how I reacted to a situation?

- **How did I handle the situation?** Did I react calmly, or did I get upset or frustrated?

- **What can I learn from this experience?** Is there something I could have done differently to feel better or handle it better?

- **What are my strengths?** What are some things I'm really good at, or enjoy doing?

- **What are my challenges?** What are some things I find difficult or want to improve on?

- **What do I like most about myself?** What makes me special and unique?

- **How can I be kind to myself and others?** What actions can I take to show kindness and understanding?

- **What am I grateful for today?** What are some things or people that make me feel happy and thankful?

- **What are my goals or dreams?** What steps can I take to work towards achieving them?

You can reflect on these questions during quiet moments, journal or draw your answers, or discuss them with a trusted adult or friend. They can help to develop self-awareness, self-esteem, and resilience.

GETTING PRACTICAL
Here are five questions you can ask yourself to grow clarity:

1. **What is most important to me?** This question helps you to understand about what matters to you, and how to make choices based on those things.

2. **What do I believe in?** This question guides you understand your values, what motivates you, and what makes your life special.

3. **What choices do I have?** By asking this question, you think about different options and the good and bad parts of each choice.

4. **What might happen if I pick this choice?** This question helps you think about what could happen after you decide so that you can choose wisely.

5. **What is the best choice for me right now?** This question supports you to combine your thoughts and make a decision that fits your goals and values.

PARTS OF ME

Seeing Clearly

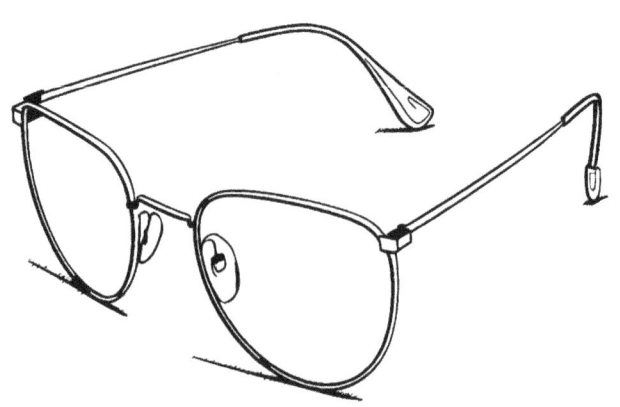

PARTS OF ME - CHAPTER 9

ASKING QUESTIONS:
The Fourth C is Curiosity

Asking Questions

Curiosity is an essential quality that helps us explore the world and learn new things. When we are curious, we are open to new experiences and more likely to approach the world with a sense of wonder and interest.

One of the great things about curiosity is that it can help us learn and grow in many ways. Whether we are exploring a new hobby, learning about different cultures, or trying out a new skill, curiosity helps us approach these experiences with an open mind and a desire to learn and grow.

Curiosity can also help us navigate difficult situations more effectively. When facing a problem or a challenge, it can be tempting to shut down and give up. But if we can approach these situations with a curious mindset, we are more likely to stay focused and interested in finding a solution. This can help us feel more empowered and less overwhelmed by the challenges we face.

Growing curiosity also helps us approach life with playfulness and creativity. Curiousness makes us more likely to take risks, try new things, and experiment with different ideas.

This can help us discover new passions and interests, and it can also help us develop our creativity and problem-solving superpowers.

A mindset is the way you think about and see the world, including your beliefs about your strengths and the possibilities in your life.

To grow curiosity, staying open to new experiences and perspectives is important. This means being willing to try new things, be interested in different cultures, explore new ideas, and challenge our assumptions and beliefs. It can also mean asking questions, seeking out new information, and being willing to learn from our mistakes.

Remember to also be curious about your inner world and your inner team, if you notice a specific part, be curious about getting to know it, and what it might want you to know.

One of the challenges of cultivating curiosity is that it can sometimes feel uncomfortable or even scary to try new things. We might worry about what other people will think, getting it wrong, or we might be afraid of failure. But the more we practice curiosity, the more comfortable we'll become with exploring new ideas and trying new things.

So how can we grow curiosity in our lives? One way is to make a conscious effort to try new things on a regular basis. This could mean taking up a new hobby, trying a new recipe, or exploring a new part of town. It could also mean seeking new information and perspectives by reading books, watching documentaries, or talking to people from different backgrounds.

Curiosity means being open to new experiences and exploring the world with a sense of wonder and interest.

Another way to grow curiosity is to see the world with excitement and interest. This means taking time to enjoy the amazing and interesting things around us and being open to the many different experiences and points of view that life has to offer - asking more questions!

Being curious about our own emotions can be very powerful. When we wonder about our feelings, like asking ourselves, 'Why does this make my angry part show up?', 'What is my sad part so sad about?', we start to understand ourselves better. We become detectives of our own minds, exploring the reasons behind our emotions. This can help us learn more about why we react in certain ways and can also help us find better ways to handle our feelings in the future.

GETTING PRACTICAL
Here are five questions you can ask yourself to grow curiosity:

1. **What would happen if...?** This question guides you to think creatively and consider different possibilities. It helps you approach situations with an open mind and consider alternative solutions.

2. **How does this work?** This question encourages you to explore and understand the mechanics behind things. It helps you develop an appreciation for the world around you and encourages you to ask more questions.

3. **What if I tried something new?** This question assists you to step outside your comfort zone and try new things. It helps you develop confidence and discover new interests and passions.

4. **What can I learn from this?** By asking this question you approach challenges as opportunities for growth and learning. It helps you develop resilience and a growth mindset.

5. **Why do my parts do things differently?** This question encourages you to think critically and consider different perspectives. It helps you develop empathy and understanding for all your parts and encourages you to approach situations with an open mind.

PARTS OF ME

Curious Creations

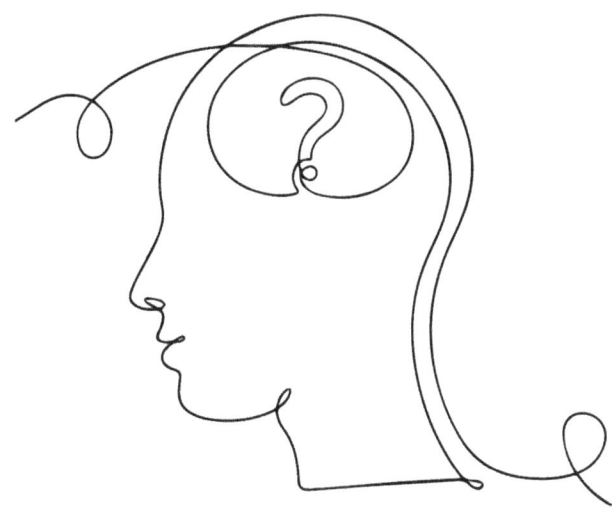

PARTS OF ME

PARTS OF ME - CHAPTER 10

BELIEVING IN YOURSELF:
The Fifth C is Confidence

Believing In Yourself

Confidence is a superpower that helps you believe in yourself and your abilities. When you feel confident, you can tap into your Self Energy, which is like the inner superhero that helps you stay calm, make good choices, and solve problems. Confidence helps you trust yourself and your inner team, which means you can work together better and handle whatever comes your way. Remember, when you believe in yourself and feel confident, your Self Energy grows stronger, and you can tackle almost any challenge!

One great thing about confidence is that it helps us take risks and pursue our dreams. When we are confident in our abilities and values, we are more likely to try new things, even if they are outside our comfort zone. This can help us discover new talents and interests, leading to more harmony.

Another great thing about confidence is that it helps us stand up for ourselves and our beliefs. When we are confident in who we are and what we want, we are less likely to be swayed by others' opinions or expectations. This can help us stay true to ourselves, even when other parts of us are angry or frustrated, and they don't understand or support us. Inner confidence can help us relate to these angry or frustrated parts, to lead us to move towards balance.

Growing confidence requires us to be honest with ourselves about who we are and what we want. It means identifying our strengths and weaknesses, being willing to take risks and pursuing our dreams, even if we are not sure we'll succeed.

Confidence means trusting our instincts and being confident in who we are and what we want, even when others don't understand.

One strategy for cultivating confidence is to practice self-compassion. Remember the first C we looked at? Compassion means Caring. This means treating ourselves and our parts with kindness and understanding, even when we make mistakes or face setbacks. By being gentle with ourselves and learning from our mistakes, we can develop greater self-confidence and resilience.

Another strategy is to set goals and work towards them in a focused way. We can build momentum and confidence in our abilities by breaking down our goals into bitesize chunks or little manageable steps and celebrating our progress along the way. One part of me might want my homework to be perfect and not be happy until is perfect, but celebrate starting it early, or handing it on time.

One of the challenges of cultivating confidence is that it can be difficult to take risks and pursue our passions, especially when other parts of us don't understand or support us. We might feel vulnerable or exposed or worry about failure or rejection. Manager parts of me might need attention before connecting to confidence for example. But by staying true to ourselves and being kind and understanding along the way, we can develop the confidence we need to pursue our dreams and live fulfilling lives.

Here's a simple exercise called 'Superhero Confidence', a confidence visualisation exercise that can help boost self-belief and make you feel more positive.

- Find a quiet, comfortable place to sit or lie down.

- Close your eyes and take a few deep breaths, inhaling slowly through your nose to a count of 4 and exhaling through your nose to a count of 4.

- Imagine yourself as a superhero with a special confidence power. Think about how you would look, what you would feel like in your body, what you would wear, and what your superhero name would be.

- Picture yourself using your confidence power to overcome challenges and help others. See yourself standing tall, in your superhero outfit, smiling, and feeling strong and brave.

- As you visualise your superhero self, notice how your body feels different. You might feel more relaxed, stronger, and more energised.

- When you're ready, take a deep breath and gently open your eyes. Remember your superhero self and your confidence power whenever you need a boost of self-belief.

This exercise helps you tap into your inner confidence and feel more capable and positive. Practice this visualisation whenever you need a reminder of your strengths and abilities. By cultivating confidence and being true to ourselves, we can take risks, pursue our dreams, and stand up for ourselves and what we believe in.

GETTING PRACTICAL
Here are five questions you can ask yourself to grow confidence:

1. **What am I good at?** This question helps you identify your strengths and recognise what you excel at.

2. **What have I accomplished in the past?** This question aids you to reflect on your achievements and recognise your capabilities.

3. **What have I learned from past mistakes?** This question guides you to learn from your experiences and identify areas for growth.

4. **What am I excited to try or learn next?** This question prompts you to focus on your interests and passions and identify new opportunities for growth and development.

5. **What would I do if I knew I couldn't fail?** By asking this you will think big and identify what you would pursue if you had limitless confidence. By exploring these possibilities, you can grow a sense of daring and boldness in what you do.

PARTS OF ME

My Strengths & Superpowers

PARTS OF ME

PARTS OF ME - CHAPTER 11

MAKING THINGS:
The Sixth C is Creativity

Making Things

Creativity is a fantastic superpower that helps us face life with playfulness and curiosity. It is all about using our imagination to develop new ideas and solutions and making things. When we are creative, we can tackle challenges with excitement and think outside the box.

Being creative is a key ingredient that helps boost our Self Energy, which is like the superhero inside us that keeps us calm, balanced, and focused. When we tap into our creativity, we connect with our true selves and allow our inner wisdom to guide us. By embracing our creativity, we strengthen the connection to our Self Energy, which helps us face life's problems with confidence and a positive attitude. Notice how all the C's are interlinked. It's hard not to talk about one C without mentioning another. So, remember, creativity isn't just about making cool things; it also helps power up the link to our Self Energy, and lets us become the superhero version of ourselves!

One of the best things about creativity is that it helps us find unique solutions to problems. By being curious and trying new things, we can see situations differently and create solutions that others might not think of.

Using creativity to explore our feelings and parts is like going on a treasure hunt inside ourselves. We can draw or write about feelings, or even act them in a play.

Creativity means using our imagination to come up with new ideas and solutions.

Creativity also lets us express ourselves in special ways. We can draw, write, make music, or do anything else that shows our ideas and feelings to the world in our own unique way. Plus, it's a cool way to see our feelings from a new point of view and learn about ourselves.

If we are facing a challenge or problem, we can use this Exercise to tap into a time we were creative: 'Creative Flashback.'

- Find a quiet and comfortable place to sit or lie down.
- Close your eyes and take a few deep breaths, inhaling slowly through your nose and exhaling through your mouth.

- Now, think back to a moment when you felt particularly creative, like when you wrote an awesome poem, made an impressive piece of art, designed a cool project, or came up with a fun game to play with your friends.

- As you remember this creative moment, try to picture it in your mind as clearly as possible. What were you doing? What were you saying? How did you feel? What sounds, smells, or colours were around you?

- Spend a few minutes exploring this memory, and feel the excitement and joy of being creative.

- Now, take a deep breath and think of a challenge or problem you're facing. Imagine using the same creativity you felt in your memory to help you find an answer or new way to tackle this problem.

- Spend a few minutes picturing how you might use your creativity to solve this problem or face this challenge, and notice how your body feels as you do this.

- When you are ready, take a deep breath and gently open your eyes. Carry the creativity from your memory with you and use it to help you tackle any challenges that come your way.

This exercise helps us reconnect to a time when we felt creative and use that feeling to boost our confidence and problem-solving skills right now in the present. We can practice this visualisation whenever we need a reminder of our creativity superpower.

To grow our creativity, we can set aside time for creative play and exploration, like drawing, writing, or learning new hobbies. We can also surround ourselves with people who inspire and support our creativity, like friends who love making art or trying new things.

Creativity is an important quality that helps us connect with our inner wisdom and express our true selves. We can feel more grounded by growing our creativity and exploring our ideas and passions.

Sometimes, being creative can feel scary because we are afraid of what others might think. But when we embrace our imagination and stay true to our passions, we can develop the creativity we need to express ourselves and live an amazing life.

Remember, creativity is a superpower that helps us face life with playfulness, curiosity, and excitement. By growing our creativity, we can solve problems, connect with others, and have a fantastic time!

GETTING PRACTICAL
Here are five questions you can ask yourself to grow creativity:

1. **What if?** This question encourages you to think creatively and consider different possibilities. It helps you approach situations with an open mind and consider alternative solutions.

2. **How can I approach this differently?** This question prompts you to consider new perspectives and approaches. It helps you break out of old habits and try new things.

3. **What would happen if I combined two different ideas?** By asking this you'll be able to experiment and combine different concepts or approaches. It helps you generate new and unique ideas.

4. **What inspires me?** With this question you can reflect and think about your interests and passions and identify what fuels your creativity. By connecting with your

sources of inspiration, you can become more creative and enthusiastic.

5. **What can I make today?** This question assists you to bring your ideas to life. It helps you build momentum and generate a sense of accomplishment, which will feel good. It is like when you start to roll a small snowball down a hill, and it gets bigger and bigger as it keeps going. That is exactly what happens when you keep trying and taking steps towards your goal. Every little step you take makes your snowball - your progress - bigger, helping you move faster towards what you want to achieve!

PARTS OF ME

Creative Expressions

PARTS OF ME

PARTS OF ME - CHAPTER 12

BEING BRAVE:

The Seventh C is Courage

Being Brave

Courage means bravely facing our fears and taking risks, even when we feel scared or uncertain. It is the strength and resilience to confront challenges and move forward towards our goals, even when it is hard.

Having courage doesn't mean we won't feel scared, but it means we are willing to push past it and do it anyway. It is about stepping outside our comfort zone, even when unsure of the outcome.

Developing courage requires us to embrace uncertainty and accept that failure is a natural part of the learning process. It is about being resilient and bouncing back when things don't go as planned.

Being brave means standing up for our feelings and acknowledging the different parts within us. It is okay to have a part that is angry, sad, or frustrated - these are all parts of who we are. When we speak for these parts, we're simply expressing our true feelings.

However, it is also important to recognise that our actions can affect others. If we realise that our actions have hurt someone, it takes courage to apologise and make things right. Remember, saying sorry doesn't mean we are weak; instead, it shows our maturity and willingness to take responsibility. It is all part of growing up and learning how to navigate the complex world of emotions and relationships.

Having courage doesn't mean we won't feel scared, but it means we are willing to push past it and do it anyway.

Think of our feelings and emotions - our parts - as a team inside of us. This team is our internal system. Now, think about what happens when the team works well together. They can play a great game, right? It is the same with our feelings. When we understand them better and they work well together, we feel happier and more confident.

But it is not just about us. When we are feeling good, it also changes how we act with our friends, family, and people at school. That is our external system. So, when we work on making our internal team stronger and happier, it also makes our outside world a bit brighter too. It is like scoring a goal for both teams at once!

Try this 'Courageous Moments Sketch':

- Gather your drawing supplies: paper, pencils, coloured pencils, markers, or any other materials you'd like to use.

- Take a moment to close your eyes and reflect on a time when you felt courageous. Maybe you stood up for a friend, tried a new activity, or faced a challenging situation.

- As you remember this courageous moment, try to visualise the scene in your mind. Think about where you were, who was with you, and what feelings you felt during that time.

- Open your eyes and start sketching the scene from your memory. Begin with a rough outline of the setting, and then add details such as people, objects, and any other elements that were present at that time.

- As you draw, try to capture your feelings during this courageous moment. Use colours, shapes, and lines to express your feelings and the scene's atmosphere.

- Once you have finished sketching the scene, take a step back and look at your drawing. Reflect on the feelings and memories it brings up for you.

- How you can use the courage you felt in that moment

to help you face challenges or fears in your current life. Is there a word that sums up the courageous moment? Keep your drawing as a reminder of your bravery and the courageous moments you've experienced.

This drawing exercise allows us to remember and reconnect with a time when we felt courageous, using a creative approach to express our feelings and experiences. The finished drawing serves as a visual reminder of our strength and bravery, which can inspire us in facing future tough times.

Courage is an essential quality that helps us confront things that have hurt us in the past. By developing our courage, we can begin to take steps towards healing and growing.

Courage means being brave, facing our fears, and taking risks, even when we feel scared or uncertain.

One way to grow courage is to practice self-compassion. Remember compassion was the first C we looked at? Self-compassion means treating ourselves and our parts with kindness and understanding, even when things don't go as planned. It means recognising that we are only human and doing the best we can.

Another way to develop courage is to take small steps outside our comfort zone. This could mean trying a new activity, speaking up for ourselves, or setting a challenging goal. By taking small steps, we can gradually build up our courage and confidence.

Courage is important because it helps us grow and learn. When we face our fears and take risks, we are more likely to discover new things about ourselves and the world around us. We are more likely to learn from our experiences and develop a deeper sense of self-awareness.

It is important to remember that courage doesn't mean being fearless. It means having the strength and resilience to face our fears, and take action in spite of them. It means being willing to take risks and learn from our experiences, even when it is hard. Sometimes it is being scared to do something, knowing we will fail or not do it right, but doing it anyway.

Growing courage requires us to believe in ourselves and our abilities. It is recognising that we have the strength and resilience to face challenges and come out stronger on the other side.

GETTING PRACTICAL
Here are five questions you can ask yourself to grow courage:

1. **What scares me?** This question helps you find out what makes you feel scared or uneasy. It shows you where you need to be brave.

2. **What is the worst thing that could happen?** This question lets you face your fears and think about the risks. It helps you see that often the scariest thing might not be as bad as you think.

3. **What if I succeed?** This question lets you think about the good things that could happen if you take a risk or face fear. It shows you the good things that can come from taking action.

4. **What would I tell my friend if they were in my situation?** This question prompts you to think kindly and understand others. It shows you that you're not the only one who feels scared, and others have faced similar challenges.

5. What small step can I take today? By asking this question you'll be able to you start taking action and keep going. It shows you that bravery often comes from small steps and trying your best.

PARTS OF ME

My Brave Moments

PARTS OF ME

PARTS OF ME - CHAPTER 13

FEELING CONNECTED:
The Eighth C is Connectedness

Feeling Connected

Connectedness is all about feeling like we are part of something bigger than ourselves. It is about feeling connected to ourselves, others, and the world around us, but it is also about understanding how we are all interconnected. When we feel connected, we feel like we belong, and we have a sense of purpose.

Connectedness helps us feel grounded and centred, even when things get tough. When we feel disconnected, we can feel lost, alone, or overwhelmed. But when we feel connected, we have a sense of direction and purpose and can handle whatever comes our way.

Cultivating connectedness requires us to approach life with an open and curious mind and be willing to explore new experiences and try new things (did you notice there's the fourth C curiosity?). It means taking the time to appreciate the beauty of the world around us and connecting with others in meaningful ways.

One way to grow connectedness is to practice mindfulness. Mindfulness means being present at the moment and paying attention to our thoughts, feelings, and surroundings without judgment. This could mean meditating, walking outside, or simply taking a few deep breaths to appreciate the world around us.

Another way to develop connectedness is to find ways to connect with others. This could mean spending time with friends and family, volunteering, or joining a group or club that interests us. When we connect with others, we build relationships, and we are more likely to feel supported and understood.

Connectedness means feeling connected to ourselves, to others, and to the world around us, and understanding how we are all interconnected.

Connectedness is an essential quality in IFS that strengthens our connection Self Energy by helping us connect more deeply with our inner selves, all our parts, and others. When we nurture connectedness, we recognise that we are not alone in our experiences and feelings and that we share common bonds with those around us. This interconnectedness makes us feel more supported, understood, and valued. As a result, we can better navigate our feelings, build stronger relationships, and create a happier inner world. Cool right?

It can be challenging to feel connected when we are busy, sad, or stressed, but taking the time to appreciate the world around us and to connect with others is essential.

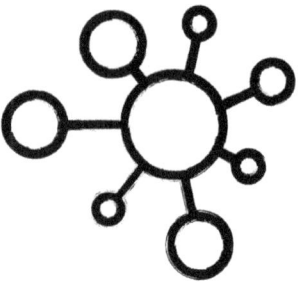

This exercise is great for noticing how connected we all are: 'My Friendship Web.'

- Grab some paper and your favourite drawing tools like crayons, markers, or coloured pencils.

- Find a comfy spot where you can draw without any distractions.

- In the middle of your paper, draw a small circle and write your name or draw a little picture of yourself inside it.

- Now, consider all the people and things you care about – your friends, family, pets, favourite activities, and special places. Draw circles around your middle circle, and inside each one, write a name or draw a small picture of each person or thing.

- After you've drawn all the circles, connect them with lines to show how they relate to you and each other. You can draw lines from your middle circle to show your connections and then draw lines between the other circles to show how they are connected to each other.

- As you connect the circles, think about how these people and things are connected to you and each other. How do they make you feel happy, supported, or inspired? How do they help each other?

- Once you've finished your friendship web, take a moment to look at your drawing. Think about all the connections you have and how they make your life more fun and interesting.

This drawing activity helps you see and appreciate all the connections in your life. By understanding how everyone and everything is connected, you can feel happier and more supported by the people and things you care about.

GETTING PRACTICAL
Here are five questions you can ask yourself to grow the feeling of being connected:

1. **Who is important to me?** By asking this you'll be able to think about the people in your life who matter to you. It shows the value of these relationships.

2. **How can I make my friendships stronger?** This query guides you think about ways to improve your connections with others. It shows you how to be a better friend and understand people better.

3. **What can I do for my community?** This question makes you think about your community and how you can help others. It shows that it is important to care for the people around us.

4. **How can I make a positive difference in the world?** With this question you can think about how to help make the world a better place. It shows that everyone can do something to make a positive change.

5. **How can I connect with nature?** This question helps you realise the importance of nature in your life and think about ways to enjoy the outdoors. It shows that we are all connected to the world around us.

PARTS OF ME

Blossoming Bonds

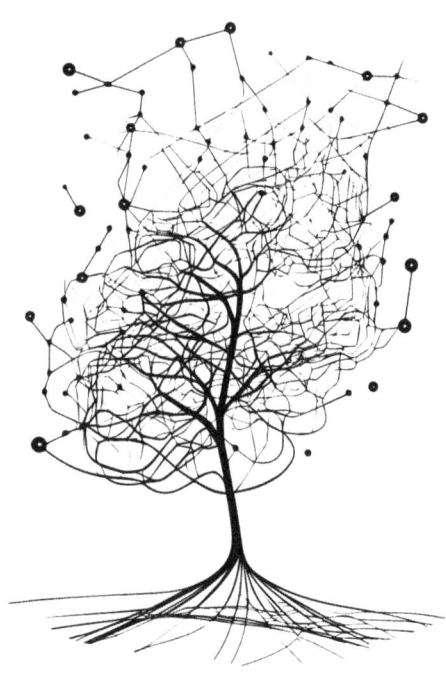

PARTS OF ME

PARTS OF ME - CHAPTER 14

THE 5 P's OF SELF ENERGY:
Let's Learn More

The 5 P's

Self Energy is the core of who we are. It is the energy within us that is always there, no matter what is happening around us. In the previous chapters, we discovered the 8C's and explored ways of growing them. Now let's meet the 5C's! They are presence, playfulness, patience, persistence, and perspective – they are the 5 P's that describe the characteristics of Self Energy in more detail:

- **Presence:** This means being fully aware and engaged in the present moment. When we are in touch with our Self Energy, we feel grounded and centred. We are able to stay focused on what's important and not get distracted by outside people, things, or situations.

- **Playfulness:** This means approaching life with curiosity and creativity. When we are playful, we are open to new experiences and unafraid to take risks. We don't take ourselves too seriously, and we are able to find joy in even the most challenging situations.

- **Patience:** This means being able to wait for things to happen in their own time. When we are patient, we don't get frustrated or anxious if things don't happen immediately. We understand that some things take time and are willing to wait for them to unfold.

- **Persistence:** This means staying committed to our goals, even when the going gets tough. When we are persistent, we don't give up easily. We are willing to put in the time and effort needed to achieve our dreams, even if it means facing obstacles along the way.

- **Perspective:** This means being able to see the bigger picture and understanding how different parts of our ourselves and our lives fit together. When we have perspective, we are able to step back and look at situations objectively. We are less likely to get caught up in small details and more able to focus on what matters.

Now that we know what each P is, let's explore each one in more detail!

PARTS OF ME

PARTS OF ME - CHAPTER 15

TAKING YOUR TIME:
The First P is Patience

Taking Your Time

Patience means being kind and understanding towards ourselves and our different parts. It is about knowing that healing and change take time. Patience and taking things one step at a time can be hard in our fast-paced world, but it is important for our happiness and growth.

In IFS, we work with our parts, which are different sides of ourselves, with their own thoughts, feelings, and behaviours. These parts might have been created because of past experiences, and some might be holding onto painful feelings or beliefs that make it hard for us to grow. When we start working with our parts, we might begin to see changes in how we think, feel, and act. However, it is important to remember that these changes may take time to happen. Being patient also helps us treat our inner parts with understanding and kindness, which makes our connection to Self Energy even stronger.

Healing can be a not easy journey that needs patience, determination, and kindness to ourselves. It is natural to want to hurry through the process and feel better quickly. But it is important to know that healing takes time, and everyone's journey is different. In IFS, we learn to be patient with ourselves and our parts, understanding that change might happen slowly. Taking our time and being patient can be hard, especially when we are used to getting quick results in other parts of our lives. Healing isn't a race, and there's no deadline to reach. The journey of healing keeps going and needs patience and persistence. With patience we learn to have realistic expectations, and be gentle with ourselves when we face tough times.

Patience means being able to wait for things to happen in their own time.

One way to grow patience in IFS is to be kind to ourselves. This means treating ourselves with kindness and understanding, just like we would with a close friend or family member. When we are patient with ourselves and our parts, we can make a safe and supportive space that helps healing and growth.

Another way to grow patience is to focus on the present moment. When we worry about the future or feel sad about the past, it can be hard to be patient. But, when we pay attention to the present moment and stay grounded in the here and now, we can find a sense of calm and 'this is ok'.

GETTING PRACTICAL
Here are five questions to help us grow patience:

1. **How can I wait without getting upset?** This question prompts you to find ways to stay calm and patient, even when things don't happen as fast as you want.

2. **What can I do to have fun while I wait?** By asking this you'll be able to you think of fun things to do when you're waiting, making patience easier.

3. **How can I remember that good things take time?** This query helps you understand the importance of patience and that waiting can lead to better results.

4. **Can I remember a time when being patient was worth it?** With this question you can think about times when patience really paid off, showing how patience can be helpful in your life.

5. **How can I stay calm and focused when I feel impatient?** This question guides you to learn skills for handling impatience and keeping a patient attitude in tricky situations.

PARTS OF ME

Taking My Time

PARTS OF ME

PARTS OF ME - CHAPTER 16

BEING PRESENT:
The Second P is Presence

Being Present

Being in the moment is a big part of IFS. It means paying attention to what's happening inside us and staying focused on what's happening right now. When we're in the moment, we can understand our thoughts, feelings, and actions better, which helps us work with our different parts in a balanced way.

Being present helps connect to our Self Energy by allowing us to focus on what's happening right now. When we pay attention to our feelings, thoughts, and what's happening around us, it is easier to understand ourselves and our different parts – our inner team.

Being present also helps us notice our feelings and our parts, making us better at handling tricky situations and getting along with people.

Plus, when we are present, we can tap into the good stuff that comes with Self Energy, like being calm, curious, kind, and connected to others. By paying attention to the here and now, we can use these qualities to make better choices and feel happier in our lives.

To cultivate presence, try practising mindfulness. Mindfulness is the practice of being fully present in the moment – in the here and now - without judgment or distraction. It involves paying attention to our breath and internal experiences while letting go of external distractions. Concentrating on what is going on inside of us, and ignoring what's going on around you. By practising mindfulness, we can develop a greater sense of calm and focus, which can help us better understand our parts and their needs.

Being present means paying attention to what's happening right here, right now.

We can also grow our presence by paying attention to our physical sensations, what our body is feeling. This means being aware of any tension or discomfort in our bodies, a clenched tummy or heart beating fast for example, which can help us better understand the feelings and thoughts that may be causing them. By paying attention to our physical sensations, we can become more present at the moment and better able to work with our parts.

It is important to remember that growing presence takes practice and patience. It is okay if it feels challenging at first, but the more we practice, the easier it will become. And remember to be kind and compassionate towards ourselves as we practice presence. Being present in the moment can be a powerful tool for understanding and working with our parts, and can help us feel more grounded and centred in our daily lives.

GETTING PRACTICAL

Here are five questions to help us cultivate presence:

1. **What am I feeling in my body right now, and where do I feel it?** This question helps you notice your physical sensations, which can make you more aware of the present moment.

2. **What thoughts are going through my mind at this moment?** This question prompts you to pay attention to your thoughts, so you can stay focused on what's happening now.

3. **What do I see, hear, smell, and feel around**

me right now? This question guides you use your senses to be more present and aware of your surroundings.

4. **How can I stay focused on the present moment instead of worrying about the past or future?** By asking this, you'll be able to learn ways to stay present, and not get lost in thoughts about what has happened or what might happen.

5. **How can I feel more connected to the here and now if I start feeling distracted or overwhelmed?** With this question you can think of ways to bring your attention back to the present when necessary.

PARTS OF ME

My Mindful Moments

PARTS OF ME - CHAPTER 17

HAVING FUN:
The Third P is Playfulness

Having Fun

Having fun is a super important part of life and a big part of connecting to our Self Energy. Being playful means having fun, laughing, and enjoying the things we do. It is about not taking things too seriously and remembering to have a good time, even when things are not so easy.

Self Energy is all about feeling calm, curious, kind, and connected to others – as we've seen in previous chapters. We can tap into these awesome qualities even more easily when we are playful. Playfulness helps us feel more relaxed and open to trying new things, making it easier to work with our inner team and our parts. Plus, when we are playful, we are more likely to have a positive attitude, which can make a huge difference in how we handle challenges.

Our inner team is made up of different parts of us, each with its feelings, thoughts, and actions. We can help these parts feel relaxed and in harmony when we are playful. This can lead to better teamwork and communication within our inner team, making it easier to work together and handle challenges.

There are some challenges to being playful, however. Sometimes, we feel too stressed, worried, or sad to be playful.

It can be hard to have fun when we are dealing with difficult feelings or situations. But that is when playfulness can be extra helpful! By finding ways to have fun and be playful, even when things are hard, we can help ourselves and our inner team feel better.

Being playful means having fun, laughing, and enjoying the things we do. It is all about not taking things too seriously and remembering to have a good time, even when things are tough.

Here are some ideas to help us be more playful and have fun:

- **Make time for fun activities:** Set aside time each day or week to do something we enjoy, like playing games, dancing, drawing, or spending time with friends. Having fun is important for our wellbeing and can help us feel more playful.

- **Try new things:** Be open to new activities or hobbies that we might find fun. This can help us discover new interests and passions while also giving us more opportunities to be playful.

- **Laugh and be silly:** Laughter is a great way to be playful and have fun. Watch funny movies or videos, tell jokes, or be silly with friends and family. Laughter can help us feel more relaxed and connected to others.

- **Connect with others:** Spend time with people who make us happy and playful. These might be friends, family members, or even pets! Being around others who enjoy having fun can also help us feel more playful.

- **Embrace our creativity:** Being creative is a great way to be playful. We can draw, paint, write, or make music to express our playful side. Plus, being creative can help us explore our thoughts and feelings in a fun and imaginative way.

- **Practice mindfulness:** Mindfulness can help us be more present in the moment, making it easier to be playful and have fun. Try taking a few deep breaths, focusing on your breath, and noticing the sounds, sights, and feelings around us. This can help us feel more connected to the present moment and more open to being playful.

- **Be kind to ourselves:** Remember that it is okay to have fun and be playful, even when things are tough. Be kind and gentle with ourselves, and remember that it is important to take care of ourselves and make time for fun.

Being playful and having fun can make the connection to our Self Energy stronger, and make our inner team work better together. So go ahead, have fun, and enjoy the awesome benefits of playfulness!

GETTING PRACTICAL
Here are five questions we can ask ourselves to cultivate playfulness:

1. **What are some fun things I love to do? How can I make sure I have time to do them more often?** This question helps you remember the activities you enjoy and encourages you to make them a bigger part of your life, increasing playfulness.

2. **Can I think of ways to make everyday tasks, like chores or homework, more fun and interesting?** This question inspires you to use your imagination to find playful approaches to everyday responsibilities.

3. **Are there any new things I want to try or learn? What can I do to start exploring these new interests?** By asking this, you'll be able to think of new adventures to embark on, making life more playful.

4. **How can I make spending time with my friends and family more fun, and full of laughter?** This query encourages you to strengthen your relationships by finding ways to bring more joy and playfulness into your shared experiences.

5. **How can I be more curious and excited about the world around me, just like when I was younger?** This question reminds you to approach life with the same sense of wonder and playfulness you had as a child, which can make everyday moments more enjoyable.

PARTS OF ME

Playful Pathways

PARTS OF ME

PARTS OF ME - CHAPTER 18

NEVER GIVING UP:
The Fourth P is Persistence

PARTS OF ME

Never Giving Up

Being persistent means that we keep trying, even when things get tough or challenging. It is an important skill to have because it helps us learn new things, achieve our goals, and grow stronger. Persistence is a big part of Self Energy because it shows us that we have the inner strength to overcome obstacles and challenges. When we are persistent, our inner team - all the different parts of us - can work together to help us reach our goals and dreams.

Self Energy is the feeling of being strong and capable. It is like having a superhero inside us that helps us face challenges and keep going, even when things get tough. When we are persistent, the connection to our Self Energy gets even stronger, and we can learn to trust ourselves more. That is because persistence helps us prove to ourselves that we can do difficult things and keep going, even when we feel like giving up.

Our inner team, all those different parts of us, play a huge role in helping us be persistent. Some of our parts might be like cheerleaders, encouraging us to keep going and cheering us on. Other parts might be like wise coaches, giving us helpful tips and strategies to overcome challenges. And sometimes, we might have parts that feel scared or worried, and that is okay too. We can learn to support and comfort those parts, so they feel more confident and ready to face challenges with us.

Being persistent isn't always easy, however. Sometimes, when we face tough situations, it can be tempting to give up or quit. But giving up doesn't always help us grow, and it doesn't teach us how to handle challenges in the future. That is why it is important to learn to be persistent and keep trying, even when we feel like giving up.

Being persistent means that we keep trying, even when things get tough.

One helpful trick is to break big goals into smaller, bitesize steps. This way, we can celebrate our progress along the way and feel more motivated to keep going. We can also remind ourselves of why we want to achieve our goals and how proud we'll feel when we finally do.

Having a friend or family member who believes in us and encourages us to keep going can help us stay positive and focused, even when things get tough. Plus, we can learn

from their experiences and use their advice to overcome our challenges.

Sometimes, we might feel frustrated or disappointed when things don't go as planned. But it is important to remember that everyone makes mistakes and faces challenges. We can be kind to ourselves, learn from our mistakes, and try again.

GETTING PRACTICAL

Here are five questions you can ask yourself to cultivate persistence:

1. **What is my goal, and how can I keep my eyes on it?** This question supports you to stay focused on your target, which is essential for persistence.

2. **When did I feel like giving up before, and what did I do to keep going? How can I use those ideas now?** This question encourages you to remember past experiences where you didn't give up and use those strategies to stay persistent now.

3. **How can I take tiny steps every day towards my goals instead of trying to do everything all at once?** By asking this you'll break your goals into smaller steps, making it easier to stay persistent and calm.

4. **How can I celebrate my small wins along the way and remind myself that I'm making progress, even when it is hard to see?** This question helps you appreciate your achievements, big or small, which boosts motivation and persistence.

5. **Who can I talk to for support and encouragement when I feel like giving up?** This query reminds you that you don't have to face challenges alone, and having support can help you stay persistent in working towards your goals.

PARTS OF ME

Keep on Going

PARTS OF ME - CHAPTER 19

LOOKING AT THE BIG PICTURE:

The Fifth P is Perspective

PARTS OF ME

Looking at the Big Picture

Perspective means looking at situations, problems, or even our feelings from various points of view. Sometimes when we are in the middle of something, it is hard to see the whole picture. But, when we take a step back and look at things from a different angle, we can gain new insights and understanding. Imagine you've just received a lower mark on a test in a new subject. You feel disappointed until you find out most of your classmates also scored low. Considering the unfamiliarity of the subject, you realise your mark is actually quite good. By shifting your perspective, you turn a potential failure into a sign of resilience, turning disappointment into motivation.

Perspective helps us see that there's more than one way to look at a situation, which can help us make better decisions and deal with challenges more effectively. When we think about Self Energy, perspective is a crucial part of it. It helps us better understand our thoughts, feelings, and actions, making working with our inner team easier.

When we can see things from different perspectives, it helps us to be more open-minded and understanding. This is a great skill to have when working with our inner team, as it helps us understand why our different parts might have their own thoughts and feelings. By looking at our parts from different angles, we can learn more about what they need and how we can work together to create a balanced inner world.

Perspective helps us see that there is more than one way to look at a situation, and that can help us make better decisions.

One challenge with perspective is that it can be hard to step back and see things differently, especially when feeling emotional or overwhelmed. We might feel stuck in our own thoughts and feelings, and it can be tough to see beyond them. However, learning to see things from a different perspective can help us feel more in control and able to handle whatever comes our way.

Above and Below

We can try a few fun activities to practice seeing things from different perspectives. One idea is to draw a picture of a problem or situation from different angles. We could draw it from above, below, or even from the point of view of someone else involved. This can help us see that there are many ways to look at a situation and that each perspective can offer new insights.

Detectives

Another activity is to pretend we are detectives; our job is to investigate our feelings or thoughts. Ask ourselves questions like, 'Why do we feel this way?' and 'What would someone else think about this situation?' By asking ourselves these questions, we can practice looking at our feelings and thoughts from different angles, helping us to better understand our inner world.

We can also talk to friends or family members about different situations and see how they might view things differently. This can help us understand that everyone has their own unique way of seeing the world, and it can show us to be more open-minded and accepting of different points of view.

Remember, it is okay if seeing things from a different perspective initially feels challenging. It is a skill that takes practice, just like any other. Be patient with ourselves and our parts, and keep trying new ways to look at things. The more we practice perspective, the better we'll become at understanding our inner team.

GETTING PRACTICAL
Here are five questions to help us see things from a different perspective:

1. **What other things might be happening that I haven't thought of yet?** Asking this question helps you think about different possibilities and understand things fully.

2. **How do other people see this situation differently than I do?** This question encourages you to consider other people's ideas, which can show you new ways to look at things.

3. **What new ways can I try to solve this problem or challenge?** By asking this, you'll think of creative solutions, which can help you see the problem from different angles.

4. **What can I learn from this situation to help me in the future?** This query teaches you to see challenges as chances to learn and grow, which can help you understand things better over time.

5. **How can I ensure fairness and kindness to all parts of me?** This question helps you think about how your other parts feel, which can help you be more caring and understanding in different situations.

PARTS OF ME

Wise Wonders

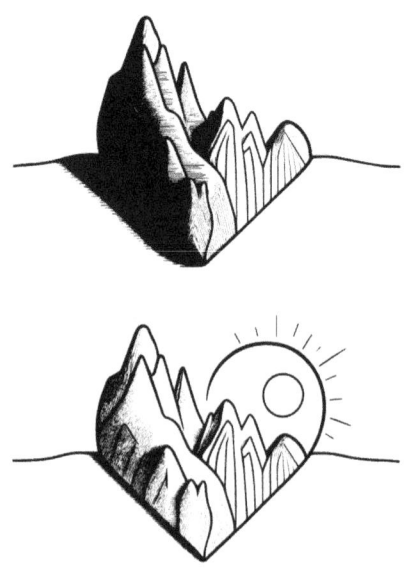

Self Energy is the part of us that stays the same, no matter what changes happen in our lives. What does change is how connected we are to our Self Energy. We have explored ways to cultivate the characteristics of presence, playfulness, persistence, perspective, and patience, so we can better connect with our Self Energy. Now let's go and meet our inner team in the next chapter!

PARTS OF ME

PARTS OF ME - CHAPTER 20

MAKING FRIENDS WITH YOUR INNER TEAM

Techniques for Working with Different Parts

In the past chapters, we learned about our inner team, the different parts of ourselves, and how important it is to understand and work with our feelings. We also talked about being in Self Energy, and how we can strengthen our connection to it. But how do we work with our inner team to create balance in our lives? In this chapter, we'll discover fun ways to work with our different parts.

Be Your Own Leader

Becoming your own leader is a cool way to work with your inner team. This means knowing and talking to your different parts and then picking which part should be in charge based on what's happening or what you want to do. For example, if you're taking a test, your 'smart and focused' part might lead the way, helping you concentrate and do your best. But if you're hanging out with friends, your 'fun and playful' part might take over, so you can relax and have a great time.

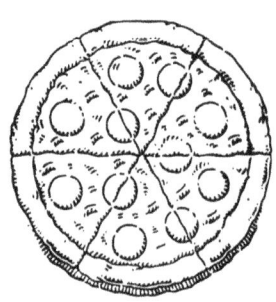

Here's a fun activity to help you get to Be Your Own Leader and know your different parts: 'Parts Wheel Exercise'

- Grab some paper and draw a big circle on it.

- Divide the circle into sections, just how you would slice a pizza. Each section will represent a different part of you.

- Label each section with a part, such as 'manager,' 'fun,' 'nervous,' 'curious,' and so on.

- Now, think about different situations in your life, like going to a party or studying for a test.

- For each situation, figure out which part would be most helpful. Your 'fun' part might be best for a party, while your 'manager' part could help with studying.

- Use your Parts Wheel as a reminder to check in with yourself and pick the best part for each situation.

As you practice this activity, you'll get to know your inner team better and learn how to be your own leader with self-awareness and kindness.

Chat with Your Parts

Another cool way to work with your inner team is to chat with them. This means pretending to converse with a specific part of you, so you can learn more about what it wants or needs. For example, if you have a 'super-perfect' part that always wants you to be perfect, you could talk to it to find out why being perfect is so important, and then work together to find a more balanced way of doing things.

GETTING PRACTICAL
Here's are some easy steps to practice chatting with your inner team:

- Find a quiet and cosy spot where no one will bother you. Take a few deep breaths and let your body relax.

- Think about a part of you that has been tricky lately; it might be a 'super-perfect' part, your 'worrier' part, or your 'trying to please everyone' part.

- Pretend that this part of you is sitting by you, it might be in front of you or next to you for example – you decide – looking like a person. Give it a name if you want.

- Start a chat with this part of you, like you're talking to a friend. Ask questions like, 'What are you trying to keep me safe from?' or 'What are you worried about?' Listen to what it has to say with no judgement.

- After you hear what it is worried about, see if you can make it feel better or find a way to work together. For example, if your 'super-perfect' part is scared of messing up, an example of what you could say is: 'I get that you want me to do my best, but sometimes it is okay to make mistakes. Let's find a way to try our hardest while still being nice to ourselves,' you'll know what to say to it to comfort it, these are your parts, and you know them best.

- Keep talking until you feel like you understand each other better or you've come up with a plan.

- Finish your chat by thanking this part of you for trying to keep you safe and reminding it that you're the one who gets to make choices and take action. Doing this activity can help you get to know your inner team better and learn how to work together. Remember to be patient and kind to yourself as you try it out.

Practising this technique can help you develop a better

relationship with your parts and work through any internal conflicts or obstacles. Remember to be patient and kind with yourself as you explore this process.

Comforting Your Parts

Another fun way to work with your parts is by giving them love and care. This means you'll imagine that you're helping a part of you that needs some extra attention. For example, if there is have a part of you that feels sad or lonely, you could imagine giving it a warm hug and telling it that you are there to help. You'll know what to say to it to comfort it, these are your parts, and you know them best. This technique, called 'Giving Your Parts Some Love,' can make a big difference to what you are feeling. By comforting your parts, you show them that you care and are ready to work together as a team.

GETTING PRACTICAL

Here's an activity to help you practice Giving Your Parts Some Love:

- Find a cosy, quiet spot where you won't be disturbed.

- Close your eyes, and take a few deep breaths to help you feel calm and relaxed.

- Think about a part of you that feels sad, hurt, or scared. Picture this part as a little person inside you who needs some help.

- Now, imagine you're a kind, loving person who wants to make that little person feel better. How would you make it feel better? What would you say to it?

- In your mind, give the little person a warm hug, and tell them some nice things to help them feel better.

- You could say things like, 'It is okay to feel sad; I'm here for you,' 'You're not alone; I'm right here with you,' or 'I love you, and I'll always take care of you.'

- Keep comforting your part until it starts to feel calm and settled.

- When you are ready, take a couple of deep breaths, and open your eyes. You and your parts will feel more grounded and cared for, and your parts will be happier too!

Practicing giving your parts some love can help you develop a deeper sense of self-compassion and self-care. It also supports you in building a stronger relationship with your inner team, remember there are no bad parts, they are all working hard to protect and care for you.

Being Present and Aware

Lastly, mindfulness is a tool that can help you work with every part of yourself. Mindfulness means paying attention to your thoughts, feelings, and what's happening in your body without getting upset or worried about them. When you practice mindfulness, you can learn to notice and accept your different parts and then decide how to act in a way that is good for you and keeps everything in balance.

GETTING PRACTICAL
Here's a fun exercise to help you practice mindfulness and work with your parts:

- Find a quiet and comfy place to sit or lie down.

- Breathe deeply a few times and let yourself relax.

- Start to pay attention to your thoughts, feelings, and what you feel in your body. Pretend you're watching them float by like clouds in the sky.

- As you notice your thoughts and feelings, try to see if any parts show up. You might find a 'worry' part making you anxious or a 'critic' part being hard on you.

- When you see your parts, be curious and open to them. Let them be there without reacting to them, just observe them.

- If you find any parts uncomfortable or upsetting, imagine yourself being kind and caring to them. For example, you might picture yourself hugging a 'scared' part and telling it everything will be fine. This is just an example; you do what feels right for your part.

- As you keep practising mindfulness, you might see that some parts start to go away or not bother you as much. That means you're working with your parts in a balanced way.

- When you're ready to finish, take a few deep breaths and return to the present moment. Remember that mindfulness is something you learn; it takes patience to get better at it.

Keep in mind that learning to work with your parts takes time, patience, and practice. But if you get better at being your leader, chatting to your parts, giving them love and care, and being aware of your thoughts and feelings, you'll create a happy inner world with all your parts on the same team.

Making friends

We learned about different techniques for working with the different parts of ourselves, but how do we get to know our parts in the first place and start building a relationship with them? Follow these steps:

1. **Pay Attention:** The first step in getting to know your parts is to start paying attention to your thoughts, feelings, and behaviours. Notice when you feel different emotions, and try to identify which part might be causing that feeling. You can even give your parts names, like 'Worry,' 'Excitement,' or 'Anger,' to make them easier to identify.

2. **Listen:** Once you've identified your parts, try to listen to them and understand their needs. Ask yourself questions like, 'What is this part trying to tell me?' or 'Why is this part showing up right now?' By listening to your parts, you can build a relationship with them.

3. **Talking:** Just like in any friendship, communication is key! Try chatting to your parts and asking them questions. You can do this in your mind or even write down a conversation. For example, you might say to your 'Worry' part, 'Hey, what's going on? Why are you feeling worried right now?' By communicating with your parts, you can start to understand them better.

4. Be Curious: Knowing your parts is a journey, so be curious and open-minded! Try to approach your parts with curiosity and exploration rather than judgment or criticism. Remember, all your parts are a part of you, and they all have something important to tell you.

By using these steps, you can build a friendship with your parts and understand them better. So, take some time to get to know your inner world; you might be surprised at what you discover!

GETTING PRACTICAL
Making Friends with Your Inner Team

Have a conversation with one of your parts that you are struggling with. Imagine that part is in the room with you, and speak to it as if you were talking to another person. Listen to what it has to say, and try to understand its point of view.

PARTS OF ME

Inner Team Chats

PARTS OF ME - CHAPTER 21

HEALING AND WELCOMING BACK HIDDEN PARTS

PARTS OF ME

Welcoming Back

Have you ever felt like there are parts of yourself that you try to ignore or push away? Maybe you have memories or feelings that are painful or embarrassing, and you don't want to think about them. Well, it turns out that these parts are important and that healing and welcoming them is essential for feeling whole and connected. These parts are called 'exile parts' and we met them right at the beginning in Chapter 2. Think of them as hidden parts, they are parts of us that carry painful memories, feelings, or beliefs we've pushed away or ignored. These parts may feel hurt, scared, or ashamed and can make us feel disconnected from ourselves and others.

By healing and welcoming back these hidden parts, we can release the pain holding us back and, as a result, feel happier in the now.

Here's why:

- **Healing:** When we heal our hidden parts, we can let go of the pain holding us back. By recognising and working through these feelings, we can move forward with a sense of freedom and lightness.

- **Welcoming Back:** After healing our hidden parts, we can welcome them back as part of our whole selves. This means understanding that all our parts belong to us and learning to work with them in a balanced way. We can feel complete and true to ourselves by welcoming back our hidden parts.

Steps to Welcome Back

So, how do we heal and welcome back our hidden parts? Here some simple steps:

- **Acknowledge:** The first step is to admit and accept that these hidden parts exist and are part of us. This might not be easy, but it is essential for the healing process.

- **Feel:** Next, we must let ourselves feel the feelings our hidden parts carry. We can do this by talking to a trusted friend or grown-up or writing in a journal. Allowing ourselves to feel these feelings helps us start to let them go.

- **Nurture:** Caring for and nurturing our hidden parts is also important. We can do this by giving them love, kindness, and understanding. For example, we might imagine ourselves hugging our hidden parts and telling them they are loved.

We can feel complete and connected by healing and welcoming back our hidden parts. Remember, it is okay to have these parts, there are no 'bad' parts: they make us unique and who we are. So, take some time to explore your hidden parts and learn to embrace them with love and understanding. But how do we actually do this? Let's discover some tools and techniques for healing and welcoming back.

- **Creative Expression:** One tool for healing and welcoming back is creative expression. This means showing your thoughts and feelings through art, music, writing, or other creative activities. Doing this lets you let go of and work through the feelings your hidden parts carry. You can then express them in a healthy way.

- **Guided Imagery:** Another technique is guided imagery, which involves imagining a safe and supportive place and bringing your hidden parts into this place. This can help you feel safe and supported while you work through the feelings your hidden parts carry.

- **Mindfulness:** This technique can help you be present and aware of your thoughts and feelings without judging or reacting to them. By practising mindfulness, you can learn to observe and accept your hidden parts and then choose how to respond to them in a way that all your inner team appreciate.

- **Self-Compassion:** Lastly, self-compassion is a tool that can help you be kind and understanding, especially when working through difficult feelings. By treating yourself with compassion and understanding, you can create a safe and supportive environment for healing and welcoming back all your parts.

Take some time to explore these tools, and find what works best for you! Remember, you are on a journey that takes time, patience, and practice. So, be patient with yourself as you explore and embrace your hidden parts, and you'll be on your way to feeling more complete.

GETTING PRACTICAL
Healing and Welcoming Back

Choose a part of you that you feel has been pushed away or ignored, and write a letter to it. Tell the part that you're ready to listen to it and understand its perspective. Be caring and understanding in your letter, and make a commitment to work with that part in the future.

PARTS OF ME

Notes Inside

PARTS OF ME

Path to Self Meditation

Find a cosy spot and start taking slow, deep breaths.
Imagine you're with your parts at the start of a path.
Ask your parts to wait there while you go on an adventure.
See how they feel. Are they scared?
Sometimes, they might not want you to go, and that's okay.
You can try again another day.

If it's okay to go, begin your imaginary journey.
If you're still thinking or watching yourself, some parts might be with you. See if they're okay with staying behind.
Do this as many times as needed.
As you leave parts behind, feel yourself becoming lighter, moving towards a space without thoughts.

You might start to feel clear, happy, and confident.
Welcome the good feelings you have into your body. Take a moment to enjoy what it's like to have so much Self inside you.
When you're ready, take a few deep breaths.
Come back to the room.

Repeat this exercise regularly, trying to remember how it feels throughout your day.

PARTS OF ME

PARTS OF ME - CHAPTER 22

GET CREATIVE

PARTS OF ME

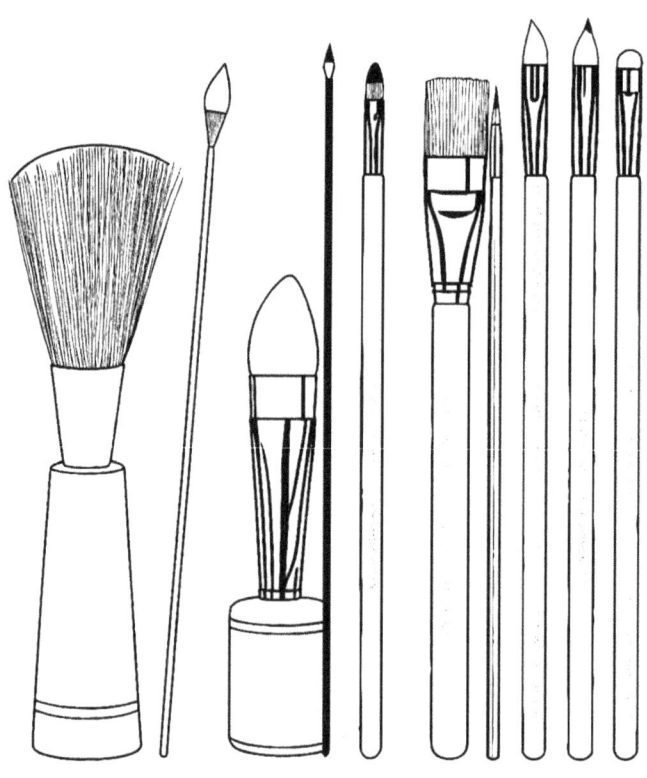

Get Creative

Only some of our parts enjoy words and writing; here are some creative exercises that will allow those other parts to express themselves.

- Draw a picture of yourself with all of your different parts. Think about how each part might be represented visually, and try to capture the essence of each one.

- Create a collage that represents your inner world. Use images from magazines or other sources that capture the different feelings and parts of yourself.

- Draw a picture of your inner crew. Imagine each part as a character with a unique personality and appearance, and draw them together in a group.

- Use different colours or textures to represent different parts of yourself. For example, if you wanted to represent an angry what colour would you use? What colour would you use to represent a calm part? Or an analytical part?

- Create a comic strip that represents a conversation between two parts of yourself. Think about how each part looks and sounds, and use speech bubbles to capture the conversation.

- Draw a picture of yourself in a safe and supportive environment. This might be a cosy room, a peaceful nature scene, or any other environment that feels safe and comforting to you.

- Create a playlist of songs that represent your different parts. Choose a song for each part that captures its essence or reflects its feelings and feelings.

- Draw a story from the perspective of one of your parts. This can help you better understand and empathise with that part and communicate its thoughts and feelings.

- Use sounds or musical instruments to represent your different parts. Record a short piece of music or soundscape where each sound or instrument represents a specific part of you, and listen to how they interact and blend.

- Design a personal logo or symbol that represents your inner world. Combine elements symbolising your different parts to create a unique and meaningful design.

- Perform a role-play or routine with a friend or family

member, acting out a conversation between your parts. This can help you explore the dynamics between your parts and how they might communicate.

- Create a 'Touch Box' for each of your parts, filled with objects representing the feelings or feelings associated with that part. This can help you understand and empathise with that part better and communicate its thoughts and feelings through the sense of touch. For example, you could include soft, comforting items for a nurturing part or rough, textured items for an angry or protective part.

- Use abstract shapes and lines to represent your different parts. This can be an abstract representation of your inner world and can allow for more creative interpretation. Remember, it is your world, only you know what it should look like!

- Design a movement or dance routine that represents your different parts. Choose specific moves or gestures that capture the essence of each part and create a sequence that allows you to express and explore the dynamics between them. You can perform this routine as a way to physically connect with your parts and gain a deeper understanding of their roles and relationships.

- Engage in a role-play activity where you physically act out a conversation or interaction between your parts. Use your body language, facial expressions, and gestures to portray the feelings and perspectives of each part.

Remember, your parts are unique to you, so there's no right or wrong way to create artwork that represents your inner world. The most important thing is to have fun, be creative, and explore different ways of expressing your feelings and parts through art, sound, and movement.

PARTS OF ME

Self Energy Sketches

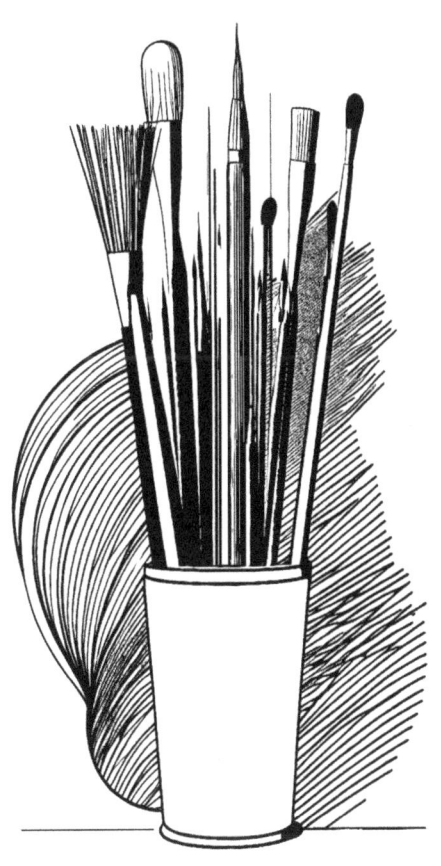

PARTS OF ME

Let's Make a Note of That

PARTS OF ME - CHAPTER 23

TIME TO PRACTICE AND REFLECT

PARTS OF ME

PARTS OF ME

Time to Practice and Reflect

Congratulations, you've made it to the end of the book about Internal Family Systems! We've learned a lot together about ourselves, Self Energy, our inner team, and the different parts that make up our inner world.

Here's a quick summary of the main points we've learned:

- We all have different parts that make up who we are. These parts can affect how we think, feel, and act, and it is important to work with them in a balanced way.

- Feelings are a big part of who we are, and it is important to understand them, and appreciate them in a healthy way.

- Self Energy is a helpful state to access our best selves. When we are in Self Energy, we can work with our parts in a more balanced and effective way.

- We all have an infinite amount of Self Energy inside us, and it's always there to connect to.

- The 8Cs are qualities we can develop to connect to Self Energy: calm, curiosity, clarity, compassion, confidence, courage, creativity, and connectedness. These qualities help us have a healthier friendship with our parts.

- The 5Ps, which are presence, perspective, patience, playfulness, and persistence, are also important qualities we can develop to work with our parts in a positive way.

- To increase the quality of the friendships with our parts, we can use techniques like leading ourselves, talking to our parts, comforting our parts, and being mindful.

- Healing and welcoming back our hidden parts can help us feel complete and connected. We can use tools like creative expression, guided imagery, mindfulness, and being kind to ourselves to help us in this journey.

We've learned a lot about our inner world and how to work with our different parts. It is time for us to practice and strengthen our IFS skills. Here are some fun exercises and activities that can help all of us:

- **Get to Know Your Parts:** Take some quiet time to think about the different parts of yourself and give them names. You can even draw or write about each part to help you understand them better.

- **Talk to Your Parts:** Choose a part you want to work with, and have a conversation with it in your mind, or write it down. Try to understand what it needs and work together to find a more balanced approach.

- **Check Your Feelings:** Throughout the day, notice how you're feeling and try to identify which part might be associated with that emotion.

- **Be Kind to Your Parts:** Choose a part that needs extra love and care. What could you do to comfort it?

GETTING PRACTICAL
Time to Practice and Reflect

Make a self-care plan that involves practising IFS techniques on a regular basis. Choose a few techniques you enjoyed or found helpful, and plan to use them throughout the week. Write down how you plan to make time for self-care in your schedule.

So, what's next for us? We encourage all of us to continue exploring our inner world and working with our parts. Try out some of the techniques we've covered in this book - see what works best for each of us and each of our inner crew. Remember, the most important thing is to be kind and compassionate and treat ourselves and our parts with understanding and love. By doing this, we can create a healthy and balanced inner world.

Thank you for reading my book, and I wish you and your inner crew the best in your journey of self-discovery and growth!

PARTS OF ME

Heart to Heart Reflections

PARTS OF ME

APPENDIX

APPENDIX:
Guide For Practitioners

Appendix: A Guide for Practitioners

The inspiration for 'Parts Of Me' arose directly from my professional experience as a therapist serving children and young adults. I recognised a gap in available resources — there were simply no books of Internal Family Systems principles in a way that resonated with a younger demographic. Guided by this understanding, I sought to contribute my own experiences and insights to create a resource that fills this gap. With this book, IFS concepts are simplified and made accessible for younger minds, providing a much-needed tool for therapists, families, and young clients alike. Having used 'Parts Of Me' with my own clients, I've witnessed first-hand its effectiveness in facilitating self-understanding and providing a novel framework for expressing emotions. It's truly rewarding to see this resource aid in their journey of self-exploration and emotional growth.

'Parts Of Me' is a friendly guide to the basics of the Internal Family Systems model, specially made for young folks. This book eases into the first four steps of the 6Fs of IFS - Find, Focus, Flesh Out, and Feel. These steps guide readers to spot their internal parts (Find), give them attention (Focus), get to know their roles and quirks (Flesh Out), and start feeling for them (Feel). The last two steps - Fetch and Facilitate - aren't covered in this beginner's guide. But no worries! The first four steps set the groundwork for any further exploration someone might want to do in the future.

Also, 'Parts Of Me' purposely skips the 'unburdening' step. Unburdening is where you let go of the tough feelings and memories that weigh a part down, and it is pretty deep stuff. It's best to have a skilled IFS therapist by your side when you get to that stage.

In my own practice, I've seen just how powerful it can be to help clients tap into their own Self Energy. There's something really special about that moment when a person discovers they have this calm, confident, and compassionate core - their Self Energy - within them. I've noticed that just focusing on this connection can create a transformative shift, similar to what happens when we go through the full 6Fs process in the Internal Family Systems model. This doesn't mean we're skipping any steps, but rather, we're starting where the impact can be the greatest for many people. It's about making therapy more accessible and seeing meaningful changes right from the start.

As therapists, we're always rooting for our clients to uncover their inner superpowers and potential to heal and grow. 'Parts

Of Me' is like a special treasure map that helps us do just that, especially when we're working with younger explorers. This book presents the deep stuff of Internal Family Systems therapy in a way that anyone can easily relate to. Here are some pointers on how you can use this book to spark magic in your therapy sessions:

- **Let the Book Kick-Off Conversations**

'Parts Of Me' introduces the cool idea of having different 'parts' of ourselves. With fun stories and neat pictures, it helps younger readers grasp these ideas in a snap. You can use these tales and images as launchpads to chat about their own parts, and how they might relate to the situations in the book.

- **Spark Self-Discovery and Understanding**

Each chapter of 'Parts Of Me' is packed with engaging activities and thought-provoking questions. Encourage your young clients to dive into these either during your sessions or as fun homework. These tasks are perfect for nudging anyone to explore their inner world, helping them understand their feelings and actions more clearly.

- **Cement Big Ideas Through Repetition**

The book revisits important IFS concepts like Self Energy, exiles, managers, and firefighters. Use it as a handy tool to keep introducing these ideas in a fun way, helping them stick and become a part of everyday thinking.

- **Make Talking Easier**

'Parts Of Me' talks in a language that is easy-peasy for anyone, not just teens. It's a fantastic helper for opening up conversations about big feelings and experiences. Encourage your clients to use the book's words to express their own thoughts and emotions.

- **Get the Whole Family on Board**

Don't just keep 'Parts Of Me' in your therapy toolbox. Recommend it for reading time at home too! Getting both your young clients and their families to read the book can help everyone understand IFS principles better. This common understanding can create a healthier communication environment at home.

- **Great for Everyone, Not Just Teens**

Don't let the teen-friendly design fool you - 'Parts Of Me' is more than a young person's book. Yes, it's perfect for young readers, with engaging stories and fun activities, but it's also a big hit with adults. It cuts through the jargon and makes the ins and outs of IFS easy to understand, no matter your age. Parents can use it to better understand their kids, kids can use it to explore their feelings, and adults looking for self-insight will of course find it handy, too.

What's even better is that 'Parts Of Me' gives everyone a shared way to talk about emotions and parts. This can really open up conversations in families and groups, helping everyone to feel heard and understood. So, whether you're a curious teen, a supportive parent, or an adult seeking self-understanding, this book has got something for you.

'Parts Of Me' isn't just a book - it's a helpful tool to start exploring your feelings, understanding those around you, and creating deeper connections with everyone. It's like a roadmap guiding us to become braver, kinder, and more curious about our wonderful, complex selves.

In a nutshell, 'Parts Of Me' is like a trusty sidekick to therapy, making the journey more exciting and easy-to-understand for our young clients. Our ultimate goal is to help them bravely explore their inner world with a sense of curiosity and kindness. With this book as a compass, we can guide them on their incredible journey of self-discovery and healing.

Further reading:

No Bad Parts: Healing Trauma and Restoring Wholeness with the Internal Family Systems Model, by Richard C. Schwartz

Internal Family Systems Therapy - 2nd Edition by Richard C. Schwartz, Martha Sweezy

The IFS Institute is a rich source of resources, books and courses: https://ifs-institute.com/

The website accompanying this book: https://partsofme.co.uk

ACKNOWLEDGMENTS

I'm deeply grateful to my husband, Tim Richardson, for his limitless support and for his big 'yes' part. This book might never have seen the light of day if he hadn't agreed that holing up in a hotel room to write for several weeks, instead of taking a traditional holiday, was a splendid idea. Throughout this journey, I've cherished his insights as a sounding board and frequent guinea pig.

A heartfelt thank you to my Mamushka, Dana Balfour. She wears many hats with grace, determination and confidence. She has shown me that one can truly achieve anything one sets one's mind to, including writing and publishing.

I extend special thanks to my step-mother, Elisabeth Ingles. Beyond her impeccable skills as an editor, proofreader, and publishing expert, witnessing the countless silent hours she's poured into her projects has inspired me deeply.

This book would be incomplete without acknowledging Fi Feehan, who has assumed multifaceted roles in my life: mentor, colleague, boss, and friend. It was Fi who first introduced me to IFS, and encouraged me to work with children, teens and young people. Fi's wisdom - across this modality and others - has been invaluable.

Lastly, most importantly, a heartfelt thank you to all my friends and family who love and embrace me and all my parts.

PARTS OF ME

PARTS OF ME

BIOGRAPHY

Calandra Balfour is a seasoned wellness expert with a BSc in neuroscience. As an accredited coach, qualified NLP practitioner, registered yoga instructor, and a dedicated sex educator, her expertise spans various dimensions of holistic wellness.

She practices as an IFS-informed, trauma-informed emotional wellbeing therapist at the wellness centre Light Before Dawn. In this role, she assists clients in replacing unproductive behavioural patterns, in a nurturing, compassionate, reassuring, and encouraging space. Light Before Dawn offers global online services, catering to children, adults, and couples. Calandra specialises in IFS, the Nervous System, Addiction, Sex, Relationships, and Children's therapy.

Outside of her therapeutic practice, Calandra is a prolific speaker, hosting talks and workshops worldwide. In addition to her wellness pursuits, Calandra owns two adult shops, emphasising the importance of healthy relationships and open communication about intimacy.

A South London (England) native, she currently resides in Brighton with her husband and two stepchildren, Kizzy and Taylor. Embracing her spirited connection with the sea, she fondly acknowledges her "mermaid part", ensuring she swims in the sea daily.